D0952724

Writer Kate Turner

Senior Editor Michael Fullalove

Art Direction and Design Sonia Moore

Senior Designer Collette Sadler

Design Assistant Philippa Nash

Nutritionist Joy Skipper

Jacket Designer Harriet Yeomans

Jacket Editor Francesca Young

Preproduction Producer
Rebecca Fallowfield

Print Producer Stephanie McConnell

Creative Technical Support
Sonia Charbonnier

Photography Will Heap

US Managing Editor Lori Hand

Managing Editor Lisa Dyer

Managing Art Editor
Marianne Markham

Art Director Maxine Pedliham

US Publisher Mike Sanders

Publishing Director Mary-Clare Jerram

First American Edition, 2016
Published in the United States by DK Publishing,
345 Hudson Street, New York, New York 10014

Copyright © 2016 Dorling Kindersley Limited
DK, a Division of Penguin Random House LLC

15 16 17 18 19 10 9 8 7 6 5 4 3 2 1
001–295020–May/2016

A catalog for this book is available
from the Library of Congress.
ISBN: 978-1-4654-5304-4

DK books are available at special discounts when
purchased in bulk for sales promotions, premiums,
fund-raising, or educational use. For details,
contact: DK Publishing Special Markets,
345 Hudson Street, New York, New York 10014
SpecialSales@dk.com

Printed and bound in China

A WORLD OF IDEAS:
SEE ALL THERE IS TO KNOW

www.dk.com

SUPERFOOD
breakfasts

Great-tasting, high-nutrient recipes to kickstart your day

CONTENTS

. . . .

Top Superfoods: Fruit p. 26

Top Superfoods: Grains & Seeds p. 34

Top Superfoods: Vegetables p. 46

Pick a recipe

Safeguard your health and give yourself the best start to the day you can with one of these 25 amazing superfood breakfasts.

Smoothies to Go
3 Ways
Page 24

Chocolate & Hazelnut
Oatmeal
Page 38

Rainbow Vegetable
Frittata
Page 50

Quinoa & Buckwheat
Granola
Page 16

Goji Berry
Rawnola
Page 18

Amaranth & Blueberry
Breakfast Bars
Page 20

Green Goddess
Juice
Page 22

Berry & Chia
Smoothie Bowl
Page 28

Tropical Fruit
Smoothie Bowl
Page 30

Apple & Kale
Smoothie Bowl
Page 32

Overnight Oats
3 Ways
Page 36

Sweet Coconut Loaf
with a Berry Coulis
Page 40

Quinoa
Superseed Bread
Page 42

Avocado, Nori &
Nut Cream Toasts
Page 44

Scrambled Eggs with
Kale & Black Beans
Page 48

Corn &
Chickpea Fritters
Page 52

Blueberry
Oat Pancakes
Page 54

Breakfast Parfaits
3 Ways
Page 56

Rice & Edamame
Protein Jar
Page 58

Why breakfast is
SO GOOD FOR YOU...

Good health begins with breakfast.
Our energy levels, mood, concentration, memory, and sleep are all affected by what we eat in the morning.

But studies show that our breakfast choices can have long-term health benefits, too: risks of obesity, heart disease, high blood pressure, and diabetes can all be reduced and our life expectancy increased by the simple act of eating breakfast. What we eat, however, is crucial.

There's no better way to start your day than with a balanced, nutritious breakfast packed with natural superfoods. These are foods that are nutrient-dense, with vitamins and minerals for the perfect functioning of our bodies. About 60 percent should be carbohydrates for sustained energy; another 25 percent should comprise healthy fats for great skin and to help fuel low-impact exercise, such as walking; the other 15 percent should be protein for building and repairing muscle.

Our bodies are hungry after the night's fast, and a good breakfast provides us with nourishment, making us feel great and helping

Orange & Pistachio Parfait

us look amazing. It also keeps us fuller for longer, so we make better choices about what to snack on and what to eat for lunch.

Research also reveals how unwise it is to go without breakfast. People who skip it will crave carbohydrates and will consume more sugary foods and beverages and less vegetables and fruit. The effects on your health soon add up.

But the best thing is that, no matter how busy you are, eating a superfood breakfast every day is easy. When you know how ...

" **Breakfast** is the secret to staying *healthy* ... studies show it can help make you leaner and **smarter** "

A superfood breakfast
EVERY DAY OF THE WEEK

If you're one of those 25 percent of people who spend less than a minute on breakfast, this book will revolutionize your life. That's because the recipes have been compiled with busy, modern lifestyles in mind ...

For when you have just two minutes to prepare ahead ...

As well as tasting great and being jam-packed with goodness, overnight oats (pp. 36–37) require just moments to put together. Simply let stand overnight to do their thing in the refrigerator and they're ready to eat (or take with you) the following day.

For chilling at the weekend ...

When time isn't an issue, breakfast can provide the chance to relax and enjoy something that is a little special. Recipes that fit the bill for a leisurely Saturday or Sunday morning include these corn and chickpea fritters (p. 52) and the blueberry oat pancakes on p. 54.

For when you have to fly, breakfast in hand ...

GOOD TO GO

We all have days when we're in a hurry, which is why throughout the book you'll find recipes flagged with the Good to Go symbol. These are breakfasts you can take with you, whether it's something you've made in advance, such as a breakfast bar (p. 20), or a smoothie (pp. 24–25) you've rustled up at the last minute. Whichever you choose, you can feel safe in the knowledge that breakfast will be superhealthy, really tasty, and guaranteed to do you good.

For feeding a young family ...

Where little ones are concerned, breakfast can be a trial, but no child could resist the pretty colors and fruity taste of the parfaits (pp. 58–59), smoothies (pp. 24–25), or smoothie bowls (pp. 28–33), which are like healthy versions of ice cream. Let them decorate the tops themselves with their favorite superfood ingredients.

What goes into a superfood breakfast?

The 25 recipes in this book are free from gluten and refined sugars. Many feature raw or sprouted ingredients and are vegetarian and dairy free. All of them are packed with natural superfoods, including:

Grains, such as oats, amaranth, and quinoa.
Nuts, such as almonds, walnuts, and pistachios.
Seeds, such as pumpkin seeds, flaxseeds, and sunflower seeds.
Fruit, including papaya, blueberries, and avocados.
Vegetables, such as kale, broccoli, and spinach.
Legumes, such as chickpeas (garbanzo beans) and black beans.

To pack that extra punch, many recipes also contain optional **nutri-boosting powders**, such as acai, lucuma, and spirulina. You'll find these in your local health-food store or online.

For a list of our favorite superfoods, turn to p. 60.

Ingredients to have
AT THE READY

Frozen fruit, nut milks, and a limited selection of seed sprouts are all available in grocery stores, but they're so much better prepared at home. One ingredient you won't track down, however, is chia preserves, but this superfood staple is easy to make.

Seed & grain sprouts

When seeds and grains sprout, their nutrient content will skyrocket.

1 Put the seeds or grains into a bowl or jar, cover with double the volume of filtered water, add a pinch of salt, and let soak at room temperature overnight.

2 In the morning, rinse well and drain, then transfer to a jar and put in a light place but out of direct sunshine. Rinse and drain twice a day. The sprouts are ready when they're as long as their source. This takes 12 hours to four days. They keep for 2–3 days in an airtight container in the refrigerator.

Frozen fruit

These are the perfect way to chill your smoothies and smoothie bowls.

1 Line a baking sheet with parchment paper and place the prepared fruit in a single layer on top. Berries can be frozen whole, but larger fruits should be peeled and cut into slices. The great thing is that you can include fruit that don't generally freeze well, such as strawberries and melon; but, because you'll be blending them in a processor, it doesn't matter.

2 Once frozen hard, transfer the fruit to sealable sandwich-sized freezer bags, label, and freeze for up to six months.

Chia preserves

As good in parfaits as in overnight oats, they can also be eaten on toast. Make them with any fruit.

1 Prepare the fruit, if necessary, by dicing it, but keep the skin on. You need about 1 cup. Put it in a saucepan with 2 tbsp maple syrup and put over medium heat for 5 minutes, until simmering.

2 Remove the pan from the heat and mash the fruit to a puree with a fork, then stir in 2 tbsp chia seeds. Lower the heat and simmer the fruit mixture, stirring from time to time, for 5 minutes.

3 Remove from the heat again, add 1 tbsp lemon juice, and decant into a jar. Put the lid on when the preserves completely cool. The recipe makes about ½ cup, which will keep in the refrigerator for a week.

Nut milk

Nut milk contains no cholesterol or saturated fat, but has plenty of healthy fats. Hazelnuts and almonds are both ideal for making nut milk. You need a piece of cheesecloth or a jelly-straining bag.

1 Soak 1–1½ cups nuts overnight in 2–3 cups of water, then drain and rinse.

2 Put into a blender or processor with 3 cups of filtered water and process for 30–60 seconds, until the mixture looks like regular milk with plenty of froth on top.

3 Put the cheesecloth in a strainer over a pitcher or bowl and pour in the milk. Let drip through, then squeeze the cloth to extract the last drops.

4 Decant into a glass bottle or jar and store in the refrigerator for up to three days.

And now

25

delicious
superfood

BREAKFAST

recipes ...

Look for the **Good to GO** logo for
breakfasts you can take with you.

GOOD
TO GO

This great-for-you granola is excellent served with nut milk and fresh fruit, but enjoy it, too, sprinkled on top of a smoothie bowl or eaten as a homemade trail mix during the day.

Quinoa & Buckwheat
GRANOLA

MAKES 8 CUPS/10 SERVINGS

1 cup raw quinoa
1¼ cups rolled oats
¾ cup buckwheat groats
½ cup sunflower seeds
½ cup pumpkin seeds
½ cup chia seeds
¾ cup unsweetened dry coconut
¾ cup walnut pieces
1 tbsp ground cinnamon
½ cup maple syrup
¼ cup coconut oil
2 tsp vanilla extract
⅔ cup raisins
⅓ cup finely chopped
    dried apricots
nut milk, to serve (optional)

1 Preheat the oven to 325°F. Line two to three large baking sheets with parchment paper.

2 Put the quinoa into a strainer and rinse under cold running water. Add to a saucepan with 2 cups water. Bring to a boil, cover, and simmer for 12 minutes or until al dente.

3 Strain and transfer to a mixing bowl. Add the oats, buckwheat, seeds, coconut, walnuts, and cinnamon.

4 In a small saucepan, gently heat the syrup, oil, and vanilla until combined. Stir into the quinoa mixture and let soak for 10 minutes.

5 Spread out to ½ inch thick on the baking sheets. Bake for 20 minutes, then stir. Reduce the oven temperature to 275°F and bake for 20 minutes, then stir. Cook for an additional 20 minutes.

6 Combine the raisins and apricots and divide equally among the baking sheets. Let cool completely, then transfer to an airtight container, or serve.

Per serving: **Calories** 495 · **Fat** 29.1g · **Carbohydrates** 49.1g · **Sugar** 18.1g
Sodium 23mg · **Fiber** 8.1g · **Protein** 11.7g · **Cholesterol** 0mg

Super *tip*
The granola will keep in an airtight container for up to a month.

A little planning is needed for this one, as it takes 2–3 days for the buckwheat and sunflower seeds to sprout, but the benefits repay the wait, because they contain high levels of nutrients.

Goji Berry
RAWNOLA

SERVES 2

1½ tbsp sunflower seeds (sprouted, about ¼ cup)

¼ cup raw buckwheat groats (sprouted, about ⅔ cup)

2½ tbsp hemp seeds

2 tbsp sesame seeds

1 tbsp chia seeds

2 tbsp goji berries

3 tbsp chopped dates

3 tbsp golden raisins or raisins

¼ tsp ground cinnamon

TO SERVE

1 cup almond milk (see recipe p. 13)

raw honey, to taste

1 peach, sliced

1 kiwi, sliced

1 Put the sunflower seeds and buckwheat groats into separate large, clean glass jars with a pinch of salt. Cover with 3½ cups of filtered water and let soak for 8 hours. Drain and rinse the contents, plus the jars.

2 Put the seeds and groats back into their jars and let stand, uncovered, to sprout for 2–3 days. Rinse twice daily in a strainer under cold running water, then return to the jars. Sunflower sprouts are ready when they're about ½ inch long; buckwheat sprouts are a little shorter.

3 Combine the sprouts, seeds, dried fruit, and cinnamon in a mixing bowl.

4 Divide the rawnola between two bowls and serve with almond milk and a little raw honey drizzled on top, if desired, with the prepared fruit on the side.

Per serving: **Calories** 407 · **Fat** 18g · **Carbohydrates** 52.9g · **Sugar** 27.6g
Sodium 12mg · **Fiber** 9.4g · **Protein** 13g · **Cholesterol** 0mg

Less well-known than quinoa, but as high in protein, amaranth adds extra crunch to these breakfast bars, which stay fresh for up to a week when stored in an airtight container.

Amaranth & Blueberry
BREAKFAST BARS

MAKES 16

1 cup raw amaranth

1 cup rolled oats

⅓ cup raisins

⅓ cup dried cranberries

¼ cup sunflower seeds

¼ cup pumpkin seeds

5 tsp chia seeds

2 tsp ground cinnamon

3 tbsp coconut oil

3 tbsp maple syrup

⅓ cup nut butter or tahini

1 small banana, mashed

1 tbsp lucuma powder (optional)

⅓ cup blueberry chia preserves (see recipe p. 13)

¼ cup goji berries

⅓ cup slivered almonds

⅓ cup pistachio nuts, coarsely crushed

1 Soak the amaranth in 2 cups of water with 1 teaspoon salt for 8 hours, then drain and rinse.

2 Preheat the oven to 350°F. Line a shallow 9 x 13-inch baking sheet with parchment paper.

3 Put the amaranth into a food processor with the oats, dried fruit, seeds, and cinnamon. Process briefly to combine.

4 Melt the coconut oil and maple syrup in a small saucepan over medium heat. Stir in the nut butter or tahini, remove from the heat, and add the banana.

5 Add to the amaranth mixture and process to combine. Spread out evenly on the sheet, pressing down with the back of a spoon. Bake for 45 minutes or until a knife inserted into the center comes out clean. Place the sheet on a rack to cool for 10 minutes.

6 Spread with chia preserves, then sprinkle with the berries and nuts, pressing them in so they stick. Let cool completely before cutting into bars.

Per bar: **Calories** 229 · **Fat** 11.9g · **Carbohydrates** 26g · **Sugar** 12.5g
Sodium 22mg · **Fiber** 4.6g · **Protein** 5.7g · **Cholesterol** 0mg

To fight off illness and give your immune system a helping hand, reach for a green goddess juice. Include the matcha powder if you feel as if your memory and concentration could use a boost.

Green Goddess
JUICE

SERVES 2

1 cup coarsely chopped spinach

⅔ cup coarsely chopped kale

1½ cups coarsely chopped celery

5 cups coarsely chopped cucumber

1½ cups coarsely chopped broccoli florets and stem

2 tbsp lemon juice

½ cup diced avocado

6 sprigs watercress

1 tsp matcha powder (optional)

raw honey, to taste

1 Press the coarsely chopped spinach, kale, celery, cucumber, and broccoli through a juicing machine.

2 Pour the juice into a high-speed blender or processor with the lemon juice, avocado, watercress, and matcha powder, if using. Blend until smooth.

3 Sweeten to taste with raw honey, pour into two glasses, and serve.

Super tip

For an extra boost of vitamin C, stir in 1 cup freshly squeezed pineapple juice.

Per serving: **Calories** 146 · **Fat** 9.8g · **Carbohydrates** 7.2g · **Sugar** 6.2g
Sodium 122mg · **Fiber** 8.9g · **Protein** 7.1g · **Cholesterol** 0mg

GOOD
TO GO

There's no easier way to load up on fruit and vegetables than with a nutritious blended drink. These meals in a jar are the perfect portable energy boost.

SMOOTHIES TO GO

· · · · · · · · · · · · · · · ·

METHOD

1 Put all the ingredients in a blender or processor and process until smooth.

2 Pour into two glasses and drink immediately, or pour into two jars, top with lids, and take them with you.

Papaya & Carrot

Dream of a flawless complexion? High levels of antioxidants in papayas will help protect your skin from damage by free radicals.

SERVES 2

INGREDIENTS

1 large ripe papaya, seeded and flesh scooped out

1 cup carrot juice (about 9 raw carrots, juiced)

1 small banana, chopped

2 tbsp lime juice

1 tsp finely chopped fresh ginger

¼ tsp ground turmeric

½ tsp baobab powder (optional)

· ·

Per serving: **Calories** 149 · **Fat** 0.4g **Carbohydrates** 38.3g · **Sugar** 28.3g · **Sodium** 68m **Fiber** 4.6g · **Protein** 3.1g · **Cholesterol** 0mg

· ·

Berry & Beet

A staple of so many detox and weight-loss plans, beets are partnered here with superfood blueberries.

SERVES 2

INGREDIENTS
⅔ cup blueberries
¾ cup raspberries
1½ raw beets (skin on),
finely chopped
1 cup spinach
1 tsp finely chopped fresh ginger
1 tsp ground cinnamon
1 cup filtered water
½–1 tsp spirulina powder (optional)
raw honey, to taste

Watermelon & Fennel

Watermelon has much to recommend itself, especially after a workout, when its amino acids will help ward off muscle soreness.

SERVES 2

INGREDIENTS
2⅔ cups coarsely chopped watermelon
1¾ cups coarsely chopped fennel
⅓ cup strawberries
1 tbsp chia seeds
1 tbsp basil leaves
1 tbsp mint leaves
1 tbsp lime juice
1 tsp maca powder (optional)

Per serving: **Calories** 73 · **Fat** 0.5g
Carbohydrates 14.7g · **Sugar** 12g · **Sodium** 69mg
Fiber 4.9g · **Protein** 3.7g · **Cholesterol** 0mg

Per serving: **Calories** 160 · **Fat** 5.5g
Carbohydrates 25.8g · **Sugar** 18.1g · **Sodium** 21mg
Fiber 9.8g · **Protein** 4.7g · **Cholesterol** 0mg

TOP SUPERFOODS
Fruit

GOJI BERRIES

Vitamins A, B$_2$, and C, plus antioxidants, selenium, and more iron, gram for gram, than steak.

BLUEBERRIES

Vitamins K and C, plus fiber, manganese, and high levels of antioxidants. Among the health claims for blueberries are that they:

- **improve** eyesight
- **lower** blood pressure
- **boost** memory
- help **protect** against cancer and heart disease

- help **protect** against cancer
- said to **prolong** life expectancy
- **boost** the immune system (which is one of the reasons goji berries are so popular with A-list celebrities)

AVOCADO

Vitamins A, C, D, and E, plus the B vitamins, potassium, monounsaturated fatty acids, and folic acid. Reputed to:

- **promote** healthy skin
- **fight** depression
- **lower** cholesterol
- **reduce** the risk of heart disease

KIWI

Vitamins C and E, plus fiber, magnesium, potassium, copper, and zinc. They can help:

- **keep** skin, hair, and nails healthy
- **increase** iron absorption
- **reduce** the risk of heart disease

BANANA

Vitamins A, B, C, and E, plus potassium, phosphorus, selenium, and antacids. Believed to help:

- **stabilize** high blood pressure
- **lift** depression
- **protect** against stomach ulcers

PAPAYA

Vitamins A and C, plus the B vitamins, antioxidants, potassium, copper, magnesium, and fiber. Said to:

- **lower** blood pressure
- **lessen** the risk of heart disease
- **improve** wound healing

PINEAPPLE

Vitamin C, the B vitamins, plus fiber, folic acid, pantothenic acid, copper, and managanese. Can help:

- **regulate** blood sugar
- **support** your immune system
- **ease** irritable bowel syndrome

COCONUT

The B vitamins, calcium, potassium, copper, manganese, iron, and lauric acid. Claimed to help:

- **prevent** strokes and Alzheimer's
- **protect** against heart disease by increasing levels of "good" HDL cholesterol

This is such a fantastic idea—take a traditional smoothie mix, make it really thick, then top it with your favorite fruit, as well as a combination of crunchy seeds or cereals. Your body will love you.

Berry & Chia
SMOOTHIE BOWL

SERVES 2

¾ cup frozen raspberries

⅔ cup frozen blueberries

1 cup nut milk (see recipe p. 13)

1 small ripe banana

⅓ cup avocado cubes

2 tbsp chia seeds

2 tbsp acai berry powder (optional)

TOPPING

½ small mango, peeled and sliced

1 tbsp slivered almonds

2 tbsp raspberries

1 tbsp pumpkin seeds

1 tbsp dried mulberries

1 Put the smoothie ingredients into a high-speed blender or food processor and process until smooth. Transfer to two bowls.

2 Lay the mango slices in a starburst pattern over half the surface, then arrange the almonds, raspberries, pumpkin seeds, and mulberries in stripes on the other half.

Super *tip*

For an intense antioxidant boost, replace the frozen raspberries and blueberries with the equivalent quantity of frozen acai berry pulp.

Per serving: **Calories** 616 · **Fat** 40.7g · **Carbohydrates** 55.6g · **Sugar** 31.5g
Sodium 35mg · **Fiber** 25.9g · **Protein** 15.8g · **Cholesterol** 0mg

For mornings when the skies are gray and you feel as if your immune system could use a boost, try this smoothie bowl, which is loaded with vitamin C and anti-inflammatories.

Tropical Fruit
SMOOTHIE BOWL

SERVES 2

1 cup frozen mango chunks

⅓ cup frozen pineapple chunks

½ cup fresh papaya chunks

1 cup freshly squeezed orange juice (or store bought)

2 tbsp hemp seeds

¼ tsp ground turmeric

1 tbsp lucuma powder (optional)

TOPPING

seeds of ½ passionfruit

½ kiwi, sliced

1 tbsp coconut flakes

1 small slice papaya, cut into chunks

1 tsp bee pollen

1 tbsp cashews

1 tsp goji berries

1 small slice watermelon, cut into chunks

1 Put the smoothie ingredients into a high-speed blender or food processor and process until smooth.

2 Pour into two bowls and arrange the toppings on the surface in stripes.

"GREAT *for* COLD *and* FLU SEASON"

Per serving: **Calories** 475 · **Fat** 22.1g · **Carbohydrates** 56.5g · **Sugar** 40.4g
Sodium 21mg · **Fiber** 8.2g · **Protein** 17g · **Cholesterol** 0mg

Almost off the charts where nutrients are concerned, kale is an obvious choice for a smoothie. If its taste isn't to your preference, don't worry—the apple is center stage here.

Apple & Kale
SMOOTHIE BOWL

SERVES 2

2 cups coarsely chopped curly kale (large stems discarded)

¾ cup chopped apple (skin on)

⅓ cup avocado cubes

1 cup alfalfa sprouts

1 large frozen banana

1 cup frozen strawberries

⅔ cup almond milk (see recipe p. 13)

1 tsp moringa powder (optional)

raw honey, to taste

TOPPING

2 tbsp blueberries

1 tsp sesame seeds

1 tbsp pomegranate seeds

3 tbsp finely diced apple (skin on)

2½ tbsp raspberries

1 tsp sunflower seeds

1 Put the smoothie ingredients into a high-speed blender or processor and process until smooth. Taste and add raw honey, if needed.

2 Pour into two bowls, then arrange the topping ingredients in stripes across the surface.

"**3** OF YOUR *five* a day for BREAKFAST"

Per serving: **Calories** 248 · **Fat** 9.8g · **Carbohydrates** 35.9g · **Sugar** 31.9g · **Sodium** 27mg · **Fiber** 8.5g · **Protein** 6.7g · **Cholesterol** 0mg

TOP SUPERFOODS
Grains & seeds

QUINOA

Manganese, magnesium, and phosphorus, plus all the essential amino acids our bodies need. Heart-friendly quinoa:

- **is gluten free** (so good for people with wheat allergies and celiac disease)
- helps **alleviate** migraine
- **relieves** constipation
- **lowers** cholesterol

FLAXSEEDS

The B vitamins, plus rich in fiber, magnesium, and omega-3 fatty acids. Studies suggest flaxseeds:

- **lower** cholesterol and high blood pressure
- **aid** digestion, thanks to their high fiber content
- **nourish** skin and hair

HEMP SEEDS

Vitamin E, plus magnesium, zinc, calcium, high levels of protein, and a powerful anti-inflammatory. They help:

- **regulate** energy levels
- **give a boost** to the immune system
- **keep** you feeling full for longer

BROWN RICE

Vitamin B$_3$, plus magnesium, manganese, and high levels of fiber, selenium, and lecithin.

- helps **maintain** a healthy body weight
- **reduces** the severity of asthma
- helps **prevent** migraines and gallstones
- **lowers** cholesterol

BUCKWHEAT

Manganese, magnesium, copper, phosphorus, and tryptophan (for a good night's sleep). Low-GI buckwheat helps:

- **prevent** energy spikes that can cause mood swings, inflammation, and weight gain
- **normalize** cholesterol levels

AMARANTH

Vitamins A and C, plus fiber, calcium, potassium, iron, and all nine essential amino acids. Amaranth helps:

- **protect** against heart disease and cancer
- **ease pain** and reduce inflammation
- **raise** energy levels
- **lower** blood pressure

OATS

The B vitamins, plus high levels of protein, soluble fiber, zinc, calcium, magnesium, and iron. Among the health claims for oats are that they:

- **keep** energy levels up
- **boost** the digestive system
- **promote** healthy skin, nails, and hair
- **improve** concentration

CHIA SEEDS

Full of energy-giving fiber, plus antioxidants, high levels of omega-3 fatty acids, and five times the calcium in cow's milk, chia seeds can help:

- **lower** cholesterol
- **stabilize** blood-sugar levels
- **improve** heart health

Stir a few simple ingredients together in the evening, then go to bed and leave breakfast to prepare itself. Overnight oats—an overnight success.

OVERNIGHT OATS

. . . .

METHOD

1 Put the base ingredients into a jar, stir gently to combine, then cover and chill overnight for about 8 hours.

2 The next morning, sprinkle on the topping ingredients, and enjoy.

Super *tip*

If warm breakfasts are more your thing, heat your overnight oats up, then add the topping just before serving.

Mixed Berries & Flaxseeds

Flaxseeds, walnuts, and goji berries make this a high-protein breakfast. The berries are rich in antiaging antioxidants.

SERVES 1

BASE INGREDIENTS	TOPPING
½ cup rolled oats	2 tbsp blackberries
⅔ cup almond milk (see recipe p. 13)	2 tbsp blueberries
⅓ cup blueberries	¼ cup raspberries
1 tbsp goji berries	2 tsp bee pollen
1 tbsp flaxseeds	raw honey, to taste
2 tbsp chopped walnuts	
1 tsp ground cinnamon	
1 tsp baobab powder (optional)	

. . . .

Per serving: **Calories** 550 · **Fat** 26.8g
Carbohydrates 62.6g · **Sugar** 25.8g · **Sodium** 13
Fiber 19.5g · **Protein** 18.4g · **Cholesterol** 0mg

. . . .

Peanut Butter, Maple Syrup & Banana

Like avocados and olive oil, peanut butter is packed with healthy fats. Include the maca to give your energy levels a boost.

SERVES 1

BASE INGREDIENTS
- ½ cup rolled oats
- ¾ cup almond milk (see recipe p. 13)
- 1 tbsp chia seeds
- 1 tbsp maple syrup
- 1 tsp maca powder (optional)

TOPPING
- 2 tbsp unsalted peanut butter
- ½ banana, sliced
- 1 tbsp quinoa and buckwheat granola (see recipe p. 16) or a good-quality, store-bought type
- 4 strawberries, sliced
- 1 tsp cacao nibs
- raw honey, to taste

Per serving: **Calories** 810 · **Fat** 38.8g **Carbohydrates** 98.1g · **Sugar** 45.2g · **Sodium** 126mg **Fiber** 20.8g · **Protein** 22.3g · **Cholesterol** 0mg

Apple, Cardamom & Pomegranate

With two great sources of slow-release energy—nuts and seeds—this marks the end for your midmorning slump.

SERVES 1

BASE INGREDIENTS
- ½ cup rolled oats
- ½ cup apple juice
- ½ small apple (skin on), grated
- 1 tbsp hemp seeds
- 2 tbsp whole almonds
- ¼ tsp ground cardamom
- 1 tsp beet powder or 1 tbsp beet juice
- 1 tsp acai powder (optional)

TOPPING
- 2 tbsp pomegranate seeds
- ¼ apple (skin on), sliced
- 2 tbsp pistachios, crushed
- raw honey, to taste

Per serving: **Calories** 630 · **Fat** 35.2g **Carbohydrates** 58.6g · **Sugar** 31.6g · **Sodium** 98mg **Fiber** 9.7g · **Protein** 21.1g · **Cholesterol** 0mg

Yes, you can eat chocolate for breakfast. Cacao is chocolate in its most natural form and packed with antioxidants and feel-great serotonin. Sometimes a little of what you crave does you good.

Chocolate & Hazelnut
OATMEAL

SERVES 2

⅔ cup rolled oats

1½ cups hazelnut milk
(see recipe p. 13)

½ large banana, sliced

2 tbsp maple syrup

1 tbsp raw cacao powder

1 tbsp hazelnuts, crushed

TOPPING

1 tbsp hazelnuts, crushed

1 tbsp cacao nibs, crushed

½ banana, sliced

maple syrup, to taste (optional)

1 Put the oats, hazelnut milk, banana, maple syrup, cacao powder, and hazelnuts into a saucepan over medium heat. Bring to a boil, stirring all the time with a wooden spoon.

2 Reduce the heat and simmer for 5 minutes, stirring often, until the oatmeal is the consistency you prefer (add more hazelnut milk, if you want it a little runnier).

3 Transfer to bowls and serve immediately, sprinkled with the topping ingredients, and drizzled with more maple syrup, if you prefer.

Per serving: **Calories** 397 · **Fat** 15.1g · **Carbohydrates** 60g · **Sugar** 40.6g
Sodium 4mg · **Fiber** 5.6g · **Protein** 7.1g · **Cholesterol** 0mg

Super *tip*

A mortar and pestle will make light work of crushing nuts and nibs. Or put into a plastic bag and smash with a rolling pin.

This needs an hour in the oven, so you may choose to make it a day ahead, but it keeps really well in an airtight container for up to a week and is delicious toasted or eaten just as it is.

Sweet Coconut Loaf
WITH A BERRY COULIS

MAKES 1 LOAF/CUTS INTO 16 SLICES

¾ cup coconut flour

½ cup brown rice flour

2 tsp baking powder

2 tsp ground cinnamon

1¾ cups unsweetened dry coconut

⅓ cup coconut oil

⅔ cup maple syrup

3 eggs, beaten

1¼ cups nut milk (see recipe p. 13)

1 tsp vanilla extract

1 cup fresh or frozen berries

TOPPING

2 cups plain yogurt

1 cup fresh berries

⅔ cup chopped walnuts

raw honey, to taste

1 Preheat the oven to 350°F. Line a 9 x 5 x 3-inch loaf pan with parchment paper.

2 Combine the flours, baking powder, cinnamon, and dry coconut in a large mixing bowl.

3 Gently heat the oil and syrup in a saucepan over medium heat, add to the flour mixture, and stir well.

4 In another bowl, whisk together the eggs, nut milk, and vanilla. Gently fold into the flour mixture.

5 Pour the batter into the pan and bake for 1 hour or until golden brown and a knife inserted into the center comes out clean. Let cool in the pan for 10 minutes, then turn out on to a wire rack to cool.

6 Put the berries into a saucepan with ½ tablespoon filtered water and bring to a boil. Reduce the heat, simmer for 5 minutes, then mash with a fork.

7 Toast the slices of loaf lightly, if preferred, then serve with the berry coulis and topping ingredients.

Per slice: **Calories** 230 · **Fat** 15.8g · **Carbohydrates** 15.5g · **Sugar** 10.3g · **Sodium** 102mg · **Fiber** 5.2g · **Protein** 5.8g · **Cholesterol** 39.6mg

Packed with protein and rich in omega-3 oils, seeds promote all-around good health. In this superfood loaf, they also add depth of flavor and plenty of crunch.

Quinoa
SUPERSEED BREAD

MAKES 1 LOAF/CUTS INTO 15 SLICES

1¾ cups quinoa

2 tbsp maple syrup

1⅔ cups buckwheat flour

1 tbsp baking powder

2 tsp salt

1 tbsp maca powder (optional)

¼ cup brown flaxseeds

⅓ cup pumpkin seeds

⅓ cup sunflower seeds

2 eggs, beaten

3 tbsp mixed seeds, to sprinkle

1 Soak the quinoa for 8 hours in 3½ cups of filtered water with 2 teaspoons salt, then drain and rinse.

2 Preheat the oven to 350°F. Line the bottom and sides of a 9 x 5 x 3-inch loaf pan with nonstick parchment paper.

3 Put the quinoa into a food processor or blender with the maple syrup and process to a smooth batter.

4 Add the flour, baking powder, salt, and maca powder, if using, and process until combined. Gradually add 1 cup of filtered water.

5 Transfer to a large mixing bowl, add the seeds, and stir to combine, then fold in the eggs. Pour into the prepared pan and sprinkle with the extra seeds.

6 Bake for 1 hour or until golden brown and a knife inserted into the center comes out clean.

7 Let cool in the pan for 5 minutes. Turn out onto a rack and let cool completely before slicing.

Per slice: **Calories** 223 · **Fat** 9.1g · **Carbohydrates** 29.2g · **Sugar** 4.3g
Sodium 336mg · **Fiber** 2.8g · **Protein** 8.1g · **Cholesterol** 25.8mg

Super *tip*

On the pages that follow are some serving ideas for this superseed bread, but it's also great with chia preserves (see p.13).

Every ingredient here plays a starring role: avocados contain healthy fats, nori is rich in minerals, while Brazil nuts have high levels of selenium to support your immune system.

Avocado, Nori &
NUT CREAM TOASTS

SERVES 3

6 slices quinoa superseed bread (see recipe p. 42) or a good-quality, store-bought type

1½ avocados, sliced

9 cherry tomatoes, sliced

3 tbsp nori seaweed, shredded

1 tbsp sesame seeds

a few sprigs basil

NUT CREAM

¾ cup Brazil nuts

2 tbsp lemon juice

1 tbsp olive oil

1 To make the nut cream, put the ingredients into a blender or processor, and process until combined. You may need to stop the machine occasionally to push the mixture down with a spatula. Gradually add 2 tablespoons of hot water to achieve a thick, creamy consistency. Season with salt and black pepper.

2 Toast the bread and spread with nut cream. Top with the avocado, tomatoes, nori, seeds, and basil.

Super tip

You can make the nut cream in advance—it will keep in an airtight container in the fridge for up to a week.

Per serving: **Calories** 929 · **Fat** 66.4g · **Carbohydrates** 62.4g · **Sugar** 11g
Sodium 692mg · **Fiber** 12.9g · **Protein** 24.7g · **Cholesterol** 51.7mg

TOP SUPERFOODS
Vegetables

FENNEL

Vitamin C, plus high in fiber, folate, manganese, potassium, niacin, calcium, iron, and phosphorus. Studies suggest fennel helps:

- **lower** blood pressure
- **prevent** damage to skin by pollution and the sun
- **reduce** the risk of heart disease and cancer

KALE

Vitamins K, A, B$_6$, and C, plus manganese, copper, anti-inflammatories, and antioxidants. Kale helps:

- **protect** against cancer and osteoporosis
- **keep** your liver healthy
- **improve** digestion

SWEET POTATOES

Vitamins A and C, plus a good source of the B vitamins, potassium, fiber, and manganese. They can help:

- **promote** feelings of relaxation
- **encourage** healthy skin and collagen growth
- **boost** energy levels without causing blood-sugar spikes

CARROTS

Vitamins A, B$_6$, C, and K, plus folate, manganese, fiber, and potassium. Carrots have been shown to:

- **lower** cholesterol
- **maintain** healthy eyes (the old wives were right)
- **reduce** the risk of cancer and diabetes

BROCCOLI

Vitamins K, E, A, B$_6$, and C, plus chromium, potassium, manganese, and fiber. Said to:

- help **lower** cholesterol and the risk of heart diesease
- **aid** detoxification
- **fight** skin damage caused by pollution and the sun

SPINACH

Vitamins K, A, B$_2$, and C, plus iron, folic acid, manganese, and magnesium. Spinach helps:

- **boost** energy and vitality
- **maintain** healthy bones and eyes
- **combat** iron-deficiency anemia

PEAS & BEANS

Vitamins K, A, C, B$_1$, and B$_6$, plus thiamin, manganese, fiber, copper, and phosphorus. They help:

- **support** your immune system
- **maintain** healthy muscles and bones
- **make** you feel full so you don't want to snack

BEETS

Vitamins A and C, plus rich in fiber, calcium, iron, manganese, and potassium. Beets are thought to:

- help **ward off** cancer
- **assist** digestion
- **maintain** healthy bowels
- **lower** cholesterol

Packed with protein and high in fatigue-busting vitamin B_{12}, eggs are among the most nutrient-dense foods we can eat. No wonder, nutritionists recommend we have one every day.

Scrambled Eggs with
KALE & BLACK BEANS

SERVES 2

½ cup finely chopped kale (thick stems discarded)

¼ cup canned black beans

2 slices quinoa superseed bread (see recipe p. 42) or store-bought alternative

1 tsp coconut oil

2 eggs

2 tbsp hummus

squeeze of lime

pinch of cayenne pepper (optional)

1 Put the kale and beans into a steamer over high heat and steam for about 4 minutes, until the kale begins to wilt.

2 Meanwhile, toast the bread under the broiler.

3 Heat the oil in a small skillet over medium heat. Crack the eggs into the pan and cook, stirring occasionally, until cooked through.

4 Spread the toast with the hummus, then layer with the kale and beans. Add a squeeze of lime, followed by the scrambled egg, seasoning, and a pinch of cayenne to taste, if desired.

Per serving: **Calories** 512 · **Fat** 20.7g · **Carbohydrates** 59.7g · **Sugar** 6g
Sodium 615mg · **Fiber** 10.5g · **Protein** 26.1g · **Cholesterol** 218.3mg

Super *tip*

If you don't have any black beans, you can use cannellini, pinto, or adzuki beans instead — they taste just as good.

A fantastic way to incorporate yet more vegetables into your day, this frittata is nutritious and delicious. It contains sweet potato, which has a low glycemic index, so you'll feel fuller for longer.

Rainbow Vegetable
FRITTATA

SERVES 4

1 tbsp coconut oil or olive oil

⅓ cup diced red onion

3 garlic cloves, crushed

½ tsp ground cinnamon

½ tsp ground turmeric

½ tsp ground paprika

2 cups finely diced sweet potato (skin on)

½ red bell pepper, finely sliced

½ cup finely chopped broccoli

⅓ cup fresh or frozen peas

⅓ cup finely chopped spinach (tough stems discarded)

⅓ cup finely chopped kale (tough stems discarded)

4 eggs

½ cup almond milk (see recipe p. 13)

1 Heat the oil in an 8–10-inch lidded skillet over medium heat. Add the onion and cook gently for 2 minutes, until translucent.

2 Add the garlic and spices and cook for 2 minutes before adding the sweet potato. Stir, reduce the heat to low, and cook with the lid on for 10 minutes.

3 Add the vegetables and a dash of water and stir well. Replace the lid and cook for 2–3 minutes, until the kale and spinach have started to wilt.

4 Meanwhile, whisk the eggs and milk together in a bowl and season with salt and black pepper.

5 Spread the vegetables evenly in the skillet and pour the egg mixture over the top. Cook without the lid for 10-15 minutes, until the bottom of the frittata has set.

6 Preheat the broiler to medium and place the skillet underneath for 4–5 minutes to set the top. Remove from the broiler, cut into wedges, and serve.

Per serving: **Calories** 187 · **Fat** 9.4g · **Carbohydrates** 17.5g · **Sugar** 5.6g
Sodium 107mg · **Fiber** 4.3g · **Protein** 9.4g · **Cholesterol** 192.5mg

An unassuming superfood, chickpea flour (or besan or garbanzo bean flour) forms the basis for these fritters. Very low in fat, it's gluten-free but high in protein, fiber, iron, and antioxidants.

Corn & Chickpea
FRITTERS

MAKES 8/SERVES 2

¾ cup chickpea flour

½ tsp baking powder

½ tsp paprika

1 egg, beaten

¼ cup almond milk (see recipe p. 13)

1 cup fresh or frozen corn kernels

½ small red bell pepper, diced

2 scallions, sliced

1 tbsp finely chopped red chile

1 tbsp chopped cilantro

1–2 tbsp coconut oil

SALSA

1 tomato, diced

1 small avocado, diced

1 tbsp chopped cilantro

1 tbsp lime juice

1 tsp finely chopped red chile

1 tsp wheatgrass powder (optional)

1 Put the ingredients for the salsa into a small bowl, stir to combine, then set aside.

2 To make the fritters, put the flour, baking powder, and paprika into a large mixing bowl.

3 Whisk the egg and milk together in a separate bowl and season with salt and black pepper. Combine with the flour mixture using a wooden spoon.

4 Add the corn kernels, red bell pepper, scallions, chile, and cilantro. The batter should be stiff.

5 Heat 1 tbsp coconut oil in a skillet over medium-high heat. Spoon 2 heaping tablespoons of batter per fritter into the pan and spread each to about ½ inch thick (you'll probably have to do this in two batches and add more coconut oil to the pan). Cook for 2 minutes or until golden brown, then turn with a spatula and cook for an additional 2 minutes.

6 Remove the fritters from the pan and serve with the salsa on the side.

Per serving: **Calories** 463 · **Fat** 26.8g · **Carbohydrates** 44.8g · **Sugar** 11.4g
Sodium 386mg · **Fiber** 8.1g · **Protein** 11.7g · **Cholesterol** 96.2mg

Super *tip*

The batter can be prepared in advance up to the end of step 3 and kept for 3 days in an airtight container in the refrigerator.

You can serve these with your favorite pancake toppings or give them a not-so-sweet twist by using shredded carrot instead of blueberries and topping with vegetables, seeds, and tahini.

Blueberry
OAT PANCAKES

· ·

MAKES 6 SMALL PANCAKES/SERVES 2

⅔ cup rolled oats

2 eggs

½ cup cottage cheese

1 tsp ground cinnamon

¼ tsp baking powder

1 tsp maca powder (optional)

⅓ cup blueberries

1–2 tsp coconut oil

TOPPING

⅔ cup blueberries

2 tbsp pumpkin seeds

2 tbsp pecans

2 tsp cacao nibs

maple syrup or raw honey, to taste

½ cup plain yogurt

1 Put the oats, eggs, cottage cheese, cinnamon, baking powder, and maca powder, if using, into a high-speed blender or food processor and process to a smooth batter.

2 Transfer to a mixing bowl, gently stir in the blueberries, then let stand for 10 minutes; the mixture will thicken.

3 Heat 1 tsp coconut oil in a skillet over medium heat. Spoon 2 tablespoons of batter for each pancake into the pan and spread to ½ inch thick (you'll probably have to do this in two batches and add more coconut oil to the pan). Cook for 3–4 minutes or until golden brown, then turn with a spatula and cook for an additional 3–4 minutes.

4 Transfer to a plate, sprinkle with the berries, seeds, nuts, and cacao nibs, drizzle with the syrup or honey, and serve with dollops of plain yogurt.

Per serving: **Calories** 803 · **Fat** 56.8g · **Carbohydrates** 42.8g · **Sugar** 19.5g
Sodium 338mg · **Fiber** 9.2g · **Protein** 31.5g · **Cholesterol** 207.4mg

If you're a fan of creamy, layered desserts, you'll love these superfood breakfast parfaits. They make any morning special.

BREAKFAST PARFAITS

• • • • • • • • • • • • • • • • •

METHOD

1 Alternate the layer ingredients for your parfait, leaving space at the top for the topping.

2 Finish with a flourish by sprinkling on the topping ingredients.

Super *tip*

On a dairy-free diet? Then use coconut yogurt in your parfaits. You'll find it in your local health-food store.

Granola & Berry

Strawberries are great for fighting fatigue, thanks to a high vitamin-C content that helps your body absorb the iron in them.

SERVES 1

LAYER INGREDIENTS	TOPPING
⅔ cup chopped, hulled strawberries	1 tsp sunflower seeds
⅔ cup quinoa and buckwheat granola (see recipe p. 16) or a store-bought alternative	1 tsp cacao nibs
⅔ cup Greek yogurt	raw honey, to taste
¼ cup blackberry chia preserves (see recipe p.13)	

• •

Per serving: **Calories** 640 · **Fat** 35g
Carbohydrates 66.6g · **Sugar** 36.4g · **Sodium** 230r
Fiber 14.7g · **Protein** 19.2g · **Cholesterol** 18.9mg

• •

Almond & Peach

or a sweet addition to this vitality-packed
parfait, swirl 1 tsp vanilla extract and 2 tsp
raw honey into the yogurt.

SERVES 1

AYER INGREDIENTS

⅔ cup Greek yogurt

½ cup blueberries

tbsp slivered almonds

2 tbsp cashews

1 peach, diced

TOPPING

a few raspberries

1 tsp hemp seeds

raw honey to taste

Per serving: **Calories** 443 · **Fat** 28.5g
ohydrates 31.4g · **Sugar** 24.9g · **Sodium** 209mg
iber 5.2g · **Protein** 17.1g · **Cholesterol** 18.9mg

Orange & Pistachio

This tangy burst of flavors will wake you up
and the high-fiber, high-protein pistachios
contain as much potassium as a banana.

SERVES 1

LAYER INGREDIENTS

1 large orange, cut into
small pieces

⅔ cup quark or
Greek yogurt

¼ cup pistachios,
lightly crushed

1 kiwi, diced

¼ cup raspberry chia
preserves (see recipe p. 13)

TOPPING

1 tsp pumpkin seeds

1 tsp chia seeds

raw honey, to taste

Per serving: **Calories** 581 · **Fat** 32.8g
Carbohydrates 56.7g · **Sugar** 44.1g · **Sodium** 368mg
Fiber 18.2g · **Protein** 19.6g · **Cholesterol** 18.9mg

Great on their own, but even better together, rice and beans provide one of the best sources of protein around (it's on par with meat). Here's to the dynamic duo.

Rice & Edamame
PROTEIN JAR

SERVES 1

¼ cup freshly cooked brown basmati rice

½ cup mixed spinach and watercress or other peppery greens

½ red bell pepper, seeded and thinly sliced

1 hard-boiled egg, quartered

1 tbsp fresh peas

1 tbsp edamame (young soybeans)

¼ beet, grated

3 tbsp hummus

2 tbsp bean sprouts

olive oil, to serve

apple cider vinegar, to serve

1 Put the cooked brown rice into the bottom of a large glass jar, then layer the spinach and watercress, red bell pepper, egg, peas, edamame, beet, hummus, and sprouts on top.

2 Season with salt and black pepper and drizzle olive oil and apple cider vinegar generously over the whole thing. Seal with the lid, grab a fork, and your breakfast is good to go.

"KEEPS you feeling FULLER for LONGER"

Per serving: **Calories** 333 · **Fat** 15.6g · **Carbohydrates** 31.1g · **Sugar** 7.2g **Sodium** 508mg · **Fiber** 8g · **Protein** 18.6g · **Cholesterol** 192.5mg

GOOD
· TO GO ·

Our favorite superfoods

Fruit (fresh)
Apples
Avocados
Bananas
Blackberries
Blueberries
Coconuts
Dates
Kiwis
Lemons
Limes
Mangoes
Nectarines
Oranges
Papayas
Passion fruits
Peaches
Pineapples
Pomegranates
Raspberries
Strawberries
Tomatoes
Watermelons

Fruit (dried)
Apricots
Cranberries
Golden raisins
Goji berries
Mulberries
Raisins

Grains & Legumes
Amaranth
Black beans
Brown rice
Buckwheat
Chickpeas (garbanzo beans)
Oats
Quinoa

Herbs
Basil
Cilantro
Mint
Parsley

Nuts & Seeds
Almonds
Brazil nuts
Cashew nuts
Chia seeds
Flaxseeds
Hazelnuts
Hemp seeds
Pecans
Peanuts
Pistachios
Pumpkin seeds
Sesame seeds
Sunflower seeds
Walnuts

Spices
Cardamom
Cayenne pepper
Cinnamon
Ginger
Paprika
Turmeric

Vegetables
Beans
Beets
Bell peppers
Broccoli
Carrots
Celery
Chiles
Corn
Cucumber
Fennel
Garlic
Kale
Onions
Peas
Scallions
Seaweed
Spinach
Sweet potatoes
Watercress

Miscellaneous
Apple cider vinegar
Bee pollen
Cottage cheese
Eggs
Maple syrup
Milk
Olive oil
Plain yogurt
Raw honey
Tahini
Vanilla extract

Nutri-boosting powders

Acai
Containing vitamins A and C, plus calcium, iron, and antioxidants, acai helps boost energy levels and support the immune system.

Baobab
High levels of vitamin C, magnesium, calcium, potassium, thiamine, and iron make baobab great for replacing the body's electrolytes after exercise. It also benefits general health.

Lucuma
A good source of vitamin A, iron, potassium, calcium, and magnesium, lucuma is low glycemic, so can help stabilize blood-sugar levels.

Maca
Maca's high levels of vitamins, amino acids, and trace minerals give a boost to energy levels and the immune system, and are good for the skin.

Matcha
Rich in vitamins A and C, plus antioxidants and selenium, matcha helps boost concentration and energy levels and lower cholesterol.

Moringa
Moringa has anti-aging properties, thanks to the iron, magnesium, zinc, and vitamins A, C, and E it contains. It also increases energy levels.

Spirulina
Exceptionally high in protein, and with a good range of B-vitamins, spirulina helps maintain eye health and improve the skin.

Wheatgrass
A rich source of vitamins A, B, C, E, and K, plus potassium, magnesium, iron, and calcium, wheatgrass aids digestion and combats the symptoms of coughs and colds.

Index

The author

Kate Turner has been creating deliciously healthy, happy food for herself and her family for decades. She loves good, honest, tasty meals that make you feel amazing, are packed full of natural energy, and are super quick and easy to prepare. Kate has a degree in health sciences and shares her ideas about food, foraging, gardening, and family life on Instagram as well as on her blog, homegrownkate.com. Other publications include *Energy Bites*, also for DK. Thanks go to her children, Stanley, Scarlet, and Tommy, for being the fiercest critics and the best taste-testing team, and to her partner Will, for everything else.